BLACKPINK

PRETTY ISN'T EVERYTHING

BLACKPINK

PRETTY ISN'T EVERYTHING

Cara J. Stevens

HARPER
An Imprint of HarperCollins*Publishers*

BLACKPINK: Pretty Isn't Everything (The Ultimate Unofficial Guide)

www.harpercollinschildrens.com

Library of Congress Control Number: 2019946016
ISBN 978-0-06-297685-7

Production management: Stonesong Press, LLC
Photo research: Heather Kemp
Text and research: Cara J. Stevens, Dinah Dunn
Typography and design: Studio 2pt0

Photo credits: Front and back cover © Christopher Polk/Shutterstock.
P. ii © Christopher Polk/Shutterstock; pp. 2–3, 4–5, 6 l © Timothy Norris/Getty Images for Coachella; p. 6 r © Scott Dudelson/Getty Images for Coachella; p. 7 l to r © Timothy Norris/Getty Images for Coachella, © Scott Dudelson/Getty Images for Coachella; pp. 8–9 © Han Myung-Gu/WireImage/Getty Images; p. 10, 12, 14, 16 © Imaginechina via AP Images; p. 18 © Yonhap News/YNA/Newscom; p. 21 © Christopher Polk/Shutterstock; p. 22 © Natt Lim/Getty Images for Coachella; p. 24 tl to bl © Rich Fury/Getty Images for Coachella; pp. 24–25 © Natt Lim/Getty Images for Coachella; p. 25 tr to br © Rich Fury/Getty Images for Coachella; pp. 26–27 © Christopher Polk/Shutterstock; pp. 28–29 © ohlee7481/Shutterstock; p. 30 t to b © Derek Teo/Shutterstock, © 501room/iStock Editorial/Getty Images Plus; pp. 30–31 bg © Lifestyle Graphic/Shutterstock, © Vector Dude/Shutterstock; p. 31 t to b © Bruce Yuanyue Bi/Getty Images, © TkKurikawa/iStock Editorial/Getty Images Plus; p. 32 l to r © Eugene Gologursky/WireImage/Getty Images, © TPG Top Photo Group/Newscom; p. 40 © Han Myung-Gu/WireImage/Getty Images; p. 41 l to r © Amy Harris/Invision/AP Images, © Scott Dudelson/Getty Images for Coachella, © ETIENNE LAURENT/EPA-EFE/Shutterstock; pp. 42–43, 44–45 t © ETIENNE LAURENT/EPA-EFE/Shutterstock; p. 44 bl, br © Timothy Norris/Getty Images for Coachella, bc © ETIENNE LAURENT/EPA-EFE/Shutterstock; p. 47 © Rich Fury/Getty Images for Coachella; p. 48 © Christopher Polk/Shutterstock; p. 50 © Rich Fury/Getty Images for Coachella; p. 53 © Raymond Hall/GC Images/Getty Images; pp. 54–55 © Timothy Norris/Getty Images for Coachella; p. 56 t to b © Jeff Vespa/Getty Images, © John Photography/Shutterstock; p. 57 © Kim Hee-Chul/EPA/Shutterstock; p. 58 © Edi Chen/Getty Images for Michael Kors; p. 59 l to r, t to b © Han Myung-Gu/WireImage/Getty Images, © THE FACT/Imazins via Getty Images, © Raymond Hall/GC Images/Getty Images, © Imaginechina via AP Images, © The Chosunilbo JNS/Imazins via Getty Images; p. 60 © Yonhap News/YNA/Newscom; p. 61 l, tr, br © Han Myung-Gu/WireImage/Getty Images, ct © Chung Sung-Jun/Getty Images for Mulberry, cb © Terence Patrick/CBS via Getty Images; p. 62 © Han Myung-Gu/WireImage/Getty Images; p. 63 l to r, t to b © Han Myung-Gu/WireImage/Getty Images, © Terence Patrick/CBS via Getty Images, © Yonhap News/YNA/Newscom, © Imaginechina via AP Images, © The Chosunilbo JNS/Imazins via Getty Images; p. 64, © JTBC PLUS/Imazins via Getty Images; p. 65 l to r, t to b © Han Myung-Gu/WireImage/Getty Images, © The Chosunilbo JNS/Imazins via Getty Images, © Julien M. Hekimian/Getty Images for Chanel, © Imaginechina via AP Images; p. 66 © Jordan Strauss/Invision for Universal Music Group/AP Images; p. 67 © Imaginechina via AP Images; p. 69 © Yonhap News/YNA/Newscom; p. 71, 72 t © Christopher Polk/Shutterstock; p. 72 b © Amy Harris/Invision/AP/Shutterstock; p.73 t to b © Christopher Polk/Shutterstock, © Natt Lim/Getty Images for Coachella; p. 74 l to r © Amy Harris/Invision/AP Images, © Timothy Norris/Getty Images for Coachella; p. 75 l to r © Rich Fury/Getty Images for Coachella, © Christopher Polk/Shutterstock; p. 76 t © Amy Harris/Invision/AP/Shutterstock; p. 76 b, p. 77 © Christopher Polk/Shutterstock; p. 78 © TPG/Splash News/Newscom; p. 85 © Terence Patrick/CBS via Getty Images; p. 86 tl © Ivanova N/Shutterstock, bl © Cynoclub/Getty Images, br © Digipub/Getty Images; p. 87 t, br © Eric Isselee/Shutterstock, bl © Digipub/Getty Images; p. 88 © Natt Lim/Getty Images for Coachella.

19 20 21 22 23 PC/LSCC 10 9 8 7 6 5 4 3 2 1 ❖ First Edition

CONTENTS

JOIN THE BLACKPINK REVOLUTION!

On July 5, 2016, K-pop fans around the world went wild when they saw the first video teaser for BLACKPINK. They had been waiting for ages for top K-pop musical hitmakers YG to launch a new girl group, and they were not disappointed.

The video opened on four stunning women in black in a dance studio. From the first beat of Rihanna's bass-heavy trap dance song, viewers knew they were seeing something special. Choreographed by dance superstar Parris Goebel, the four members of BLACKPINK—Rosé, Lisa, Jisoo, and Jennie—moved like they had been together for years, which they had.

While they didn't sing a note, BLACKPINK were obviously stars. A little more than a month later, their debut single album *Square One* proved it.

Since their remarkable debut, the women of BLACKPINK have been topping charts and stealing hearts. With their diverse personalities, origin stories, and unique singing, dancing, and fashion styles, BLACKPINK has been giving fans lots to love about their girl crushes. Each song, each appearance, and each moment caught on camera showcases a new side of these complex, fashionable, and oh-so-accessible idols.

Learn more about the history, talent, and hard work that made this group of "instant sisters," who love to sing and dance as much as they adore their terrific fans, the BLINKS.

<An "idol" in K-pop is an artist who trained for years and has a successful debut and devoted fans.>

The Story Behind the Name

The name BLACKPINK refers to how the members' sweet, feminine side mixes with a tough, edgy attitude. "Pink is commonly used to portray prettiness, but BLACKPINK actually means to say that: 'pretty isn't everything,'" explained a representative of YG Entertainment, the company that formed the group and manages them. "It also symbolizes that they are a team that encompasses not only beauty, but also great talent."

The Story Behind the Lightstick

BLACKPINK's unique combination of sweet and edgy shines through every aspect of their being: their fashion choices, their singing style, and even their fan lightstick—a pink hammer—which is both pretty and dangerous at the same time. The strength of these girls underneath their appearance challenges what people think women can be and encourages listeners to look beyond appearances.

True fans wave the official BLACKPINK pink and black light-up hammers at concerts and appearances to show their support.

Jisoo said in a 2018 V Live that it was difficult to figure out what their lightstick should be "because there are male fans, as well as female fans. For people of all ages and men and women alike, we wanted a design that would work for everyone."

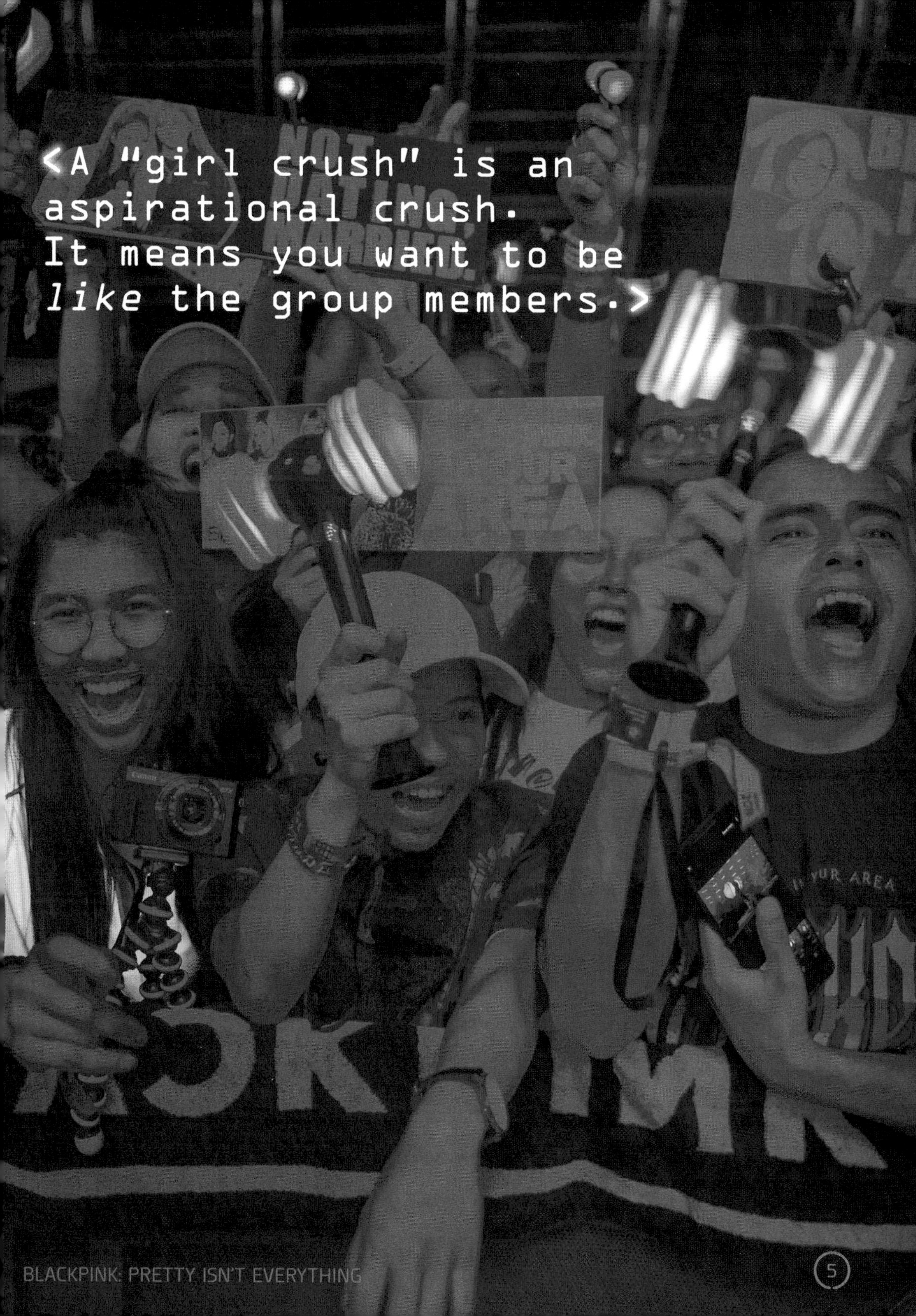

<A "girl crush" is an aspirational crush.
It means you want to be *like* the group members.>

ABOUT THE IDOLS

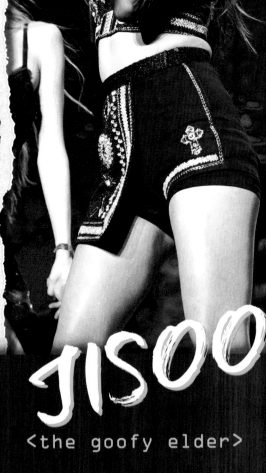

LISA

<the free spirit>

JISOO

<the goofy elder>

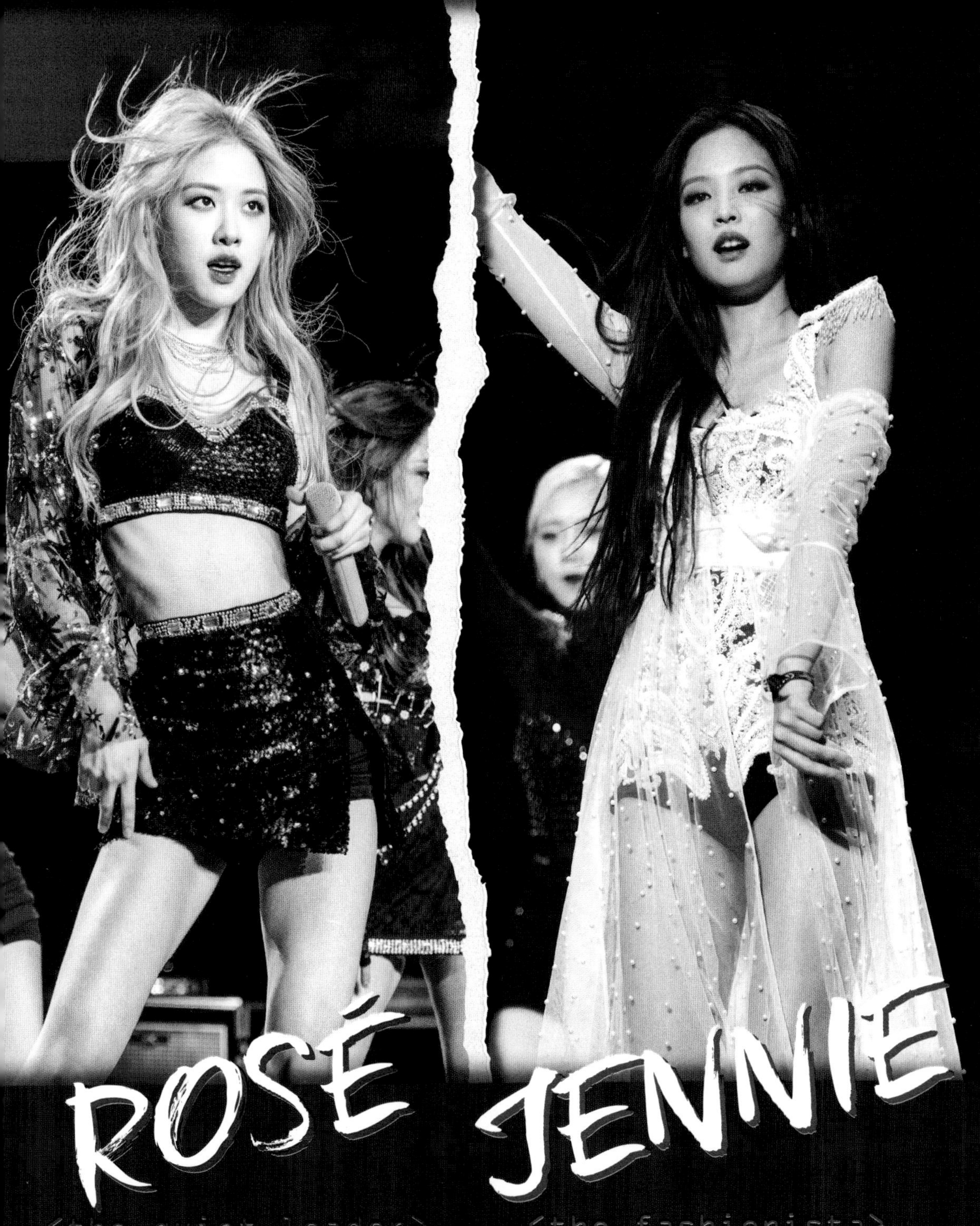

ROSÉ

<the quiet leader>

JENNIE

<the fashionista>

BLACKPINK: THE MUSIC

These twentysomething idols are taking the world by storm, one heart-thumping beat at a time. BLACKPINK's music is a fusion of loud, electropop beats combined with pop melodies and explosive rapping, underscored by confident dance moves. Working with YG producer Teddy Park, they have a genre-bending sound that keeps listeners and viewers on their toes. Their songs range from soft, acoustic ballads to edgy pop-R&B to catchy dance songs.

Lisa told the music magazine *Billboard* that she credits their intensive training process with helping the members develop their different styles: "We all tried rapping, we all tried singing, we all tried different kinds of styles and performances, so we naturally found our perfect spot."

K-pop music features a fusion of multiple styles, including EDM, hip-hop, rock, R&B, and rap. K-pop songs are usually accompanied by tight choreography and striking dance moves. The cinematic music videos (MVs) are filled with symbolism, filmed in multiple locations with many costume changes, and often have a dramatic story line.

MEMBER PROFILES AND BIOS

Jisoo

(Kim Ji-Soo / 지수)

Role: Lead vocalist, Unni (eldest)

Birthplace: South Korea

Birthday: January 3, 1995

Zodiac sign: Capricorn

Animal sign: Year of the Pig

Languages spoken: Korean, Japanese, Chinese (Jisoo understands English, but she is often too shy to speak it in public.)

Favorite things: Playing video games, balancing things on her head, trying new foods

Personality: 4D

Nicknames: Chi Choo, Jichu

Signed as a trainee: July 2011

Fun fact: Jisoo believes in ghosts. She believes she has had many encounters with the spirit world. She and Lisa both agree there may have been a ghost living in the wardrobe room of their trainee house!

> The term "4D" is Korean slang used to describe someone who has a unique personality.

When she was young, Jisoo loved singing in front of her family. They encouraged her to audition for YG Entertainment. In 2011, at the age of 16, Jisoo became a trainee studying music and performance. She also plays traditional South Korean drums.

In January of 2013, YG announced that Jisoo would be the first official member of their upcoming girl group. She is the Unni, or eldest member, and BLACKPINK's "visual." In K-pop terms, this means she is the official "face" of the group. The visual of a K-pop group often gets offered starring roles in TV shows, fellow artists' MVs, commercials, and sponsored advertisements—and Jisoo is no exception. She appeared in Epik High's "Spoiler" and "Happen Ending" in 2014; Hi Soohyun's MV "I'm Different;" and in the South Korean TV drama *Producer*.

Jisoo is considered the 4D of the group because of her quirky personality and goofy antics on- and off-camera. Although she is also the eldest member of the group, she is the maknae (youngest) sibling in her own family. Jisoo doesn't share much publicly about her parents or her older brother and sister.

Jisoo loves to play games. She and Jennie can often be found playing *Overwatch* together. Jisoo even got her own gaming room in the BLACKPINK vacation house. Lisa is always after Jisoo to lay off the video games, but Jisoo defends her right to play.

Jisoo's favorite BLACKPINK song is "Forever Young." She told* Billboard, *"Every time I listen to it, it refreshes me. Whenever I'm down, it makes me happy."

Jennie

(Kim Jennie / 제니)

Role: Rapper, Vocalist

Birthplace: South Korea, but she spent five years in New Zealand

Birthday: January 16, 1996

Zodiac sign: Capricorn

Animal sign: Year of the Rat

Languages spoken: Korean, English, and Japanese

Favorite things: Jennie loves animals! She has a white cocker spaniel named Kai and a brown Pomeranian named Kuma. She also loves to cook and enjoys making crafts.

Personality: Bubbly, aegyo (cute)

Nicknames: Human Chanel, YG Princess

Signed as a trainee: August 2010

Fun fact: For Jennie's birthday in 2018, BLINKS across the world tweeted #shiningjennieday, making it a top ten hashtag! One dedicated fan even sprang for a costly billboard takeover in Times Square!

Jennie is a trend-setting fashionista with impeccable style. As fans know, she loves Chanel so much that she became a brand ambassador for Chanel Korea in 2018. Lisa and Jennie both love clothes: "We can't go shopping together," said Jennie in an interview with *Billboard*. "We are no good for each other. We can't stop each other."

An only child, Jennie was ten years old when her parents sent her to New Zealand to study abroad. There she became fluent in English. After a few years, Jennie's mom took her to Florida to enroll in a new school. But Jennie had other dreams—she wanted to learn how to sing, dance, and become an entertainer. She told her mother, "Instead of going to a new school, why don't I come home and do something I want to do for the rest of my life?"

After auditioning for YG Entertainment, she became a trainee in 2010 at age fourteen. Because she was fluent in English and could speak quickly, YG helped her focus on her rapping skills. She became well-known as a trainee after an appearance in G-Dragon's music video and appeared in several other MVs before she debuted with BLACKPINK.

Jennie was the first BLACKPINK member to release her own single, "SOLO," in 2019. The ode to being self-reliant debuted at #3 on *Billboard*'s World Digital Song Sales chart, soon rising to #1. YG plans on rolling out solo projects for all of the members, which Jennie believes strengthens them as a group as "it allows us to expand our music range," she told the Hollywood Reporter. "And so, as all of our members have their own personality, taste in music, and style, it'll be great if we can showcase all of our individual strengths through these solo projects."

Jennie's favorite BLACKPINK song is "Ddu-Du Ddu-Du." She told **Billboard***, **"That song brought back my confidence—fans will support you no matter what you do, as long as you enjoy it, and I like what I'm doing."***

Rosé

(Park Chaeyoung / Roseanne Park / 박채영)

Role: Main vocalist
Birthplace: New Zealand, but she was raised in Australia
Birthday: February 11, 1997
Zodiac sign: Aquarius
Animal sign: Year of the Ox
Languages spoken: English, Korean, and Japanese
Favorite things: Singing, playing piano and guitar, drawing
Personality: Shy
Nicknames: Rosie, Pasta
Signed as a trainee: May 2012
Fun fact: She has five ear piercings, but no tattoos, because YG artists are not allowed to get them.

Rosé was born in New Zealand and moved to Melbourne, Australia, when she was seven years old. From a young age, Rosé had a passion for music. She grew up singing in her room, accompanying herself on guitar. "In Australia, I didn't think that there was much of a chance for me to become a singer—especially to become a K-pop star . . . I was living so far from the country that it never really occurred to me as a possibility," she told the *Sydney Morning Herald*.

When her dad heard YG was holding open auditions in Australia in 2012, he suggested she try out. Her mother disagreed, which led to several heated family arguments about whether or not she should go. Ultimately Rosé's parents bought her a ticket and she flew across the country to Sydney to audition. The competition was fierce, but Rosé's sweet, earnest voice and beauty earned her the top spot in the auditions. Within two months, at age sixteen, she left home to live in the dorms in South Korea and joined YG as a trainee.

The group has fond memories of first meeting their final member. "Rosé joined us last. She came through with her guitar, this little girl from Australia, and we just clicked," said Jennie during an interview with Zach Sang. "We started singing together from day one." Rosé laughed, adding, "We ended up jamming until like five a.m." And they have been jamming ever since!

Rosé's favorite BLACKPINK song is "Playing with Fire." She told* Billboard, *"It covers the warmth of me, and it's also not so hard-core—it's pop, but it's nice and warm and dark."

Lisa

(Lalisa / Pranpriya Manoban / 리사)

Role: Main Dancer, Lead Rapper, Vocalist, Maknae (youngest)
Birthplace: Bangkok, Thailand
Birthday: March 27, 1997
Zodiac sign: Aries
Animal sign: Year of the Ox
Languages spoken: Korean, English, Japanese, Thai, and a little Chinese
Favorite things: Makeup, photography, Nintendo games
Personality: Stylish and sophisticated, but also mischievous and goofy at times
Nicknames: Lallice, Nallalisa, Jolisa, Laliz, Pokpak
Signed as a trainee: April 2011
Fun fact: Lisa's birth name was Pranpriya, but she changed her name to Lalisa after having her fortune told. Lalisa means "one who is praised" in the Thai language.

Lisa's favorite BLACKPINK song is "Whistle." She told Billboard, "I love hip-hop, and it's hip-hop based, so I think it's just me."

Born and raised in Thailand, Lisa grew up obsessed with hip-hop and dancing. Her career took off when she was fourteen after she attended a YG audition in Thailand. As YG's first nonKorean trainee, Lisa barely spoke a word of Korean when she arrived at the dorm. Her fellow trainees helped her learn the language. That's where she also learned to rap.

Lisa is close with her parents. Her stepfather, originally from Switzerland, runs a culinary school in Thailand, which could explain Lisa's love of all kinds of food. Her parents visited during an episode of the band's reality show, *BLACKPINK House*. The girls enjoyed spending time with Lisa's family, especially when her parents cooked for them. When asked what makes her happy, Lisa said, "Talking with my mom on the phone every day! Seeing me work hard makes her happy, and seeing that gives me strength."

Before she debuted with BLACKPINK, Lisa appeared as a dancer in several music videos and was a model for YG's street fashion brand NONA9ON.

With her cool street style and infectious smile, Lisa is the most followed K-pop idol on Instagram. When she learned that, Lisa was surprised. "I couldn't believe it. I was like, what? No way!" While millions admire her style, her fellow members know her as a goofball. "Lisa is so charismatic on the stage, but she's actually like a little brother, not even a little sister, when not on the stage," said Jisoo. "She is so mischievous and cute, like a little child."

"Lisa makes a lot of jokes. She's like the class clown."
—Rosé

YG ENTERTAINMENT

The YG Family Patriarch – Yang Hyun Suk

Yang Hyun Suk began in the music industry as a member of the award-winning Seo Taiji and Boys, a pop group that helped pioneer the use of rap in Korean music. They had massive success with hits such as "I Know" (1992) and "Come Back Home" (1995). When the band broke up in 1996, Hyun Suk established YG Entertainment and produced albums by artists including BIGBANG, Se7en, and Psy, whose hit "Gangnam Style" was the first to rack up one billion views. "Gangnam Style" was the most watched video in YouTube history until Wiz Khalifa and Charlie Puth's song "See You Again" stole the spotlight on July 10, 2017. In 2019, however, Hyun Suk resigned from YG, due to an ongoing scandal.

YG Entertainment has expanded to become a record label, talent agency, music production company, event management and concert production company, and music publishing house. It is also one of the companies in Korea that creates pop groups and stars such as BLACKPINK. In the K-pop world, these companies recruit, train, cast, debut, feature, and manage all aspects of each idol's career, public image, and even their private life. The company helps the idols land modeling and sponsorship contracts, create licensed games and products, manage appearances around the world, produce music videos, and land starring roles in online and broadcast video programs.

"Until now, I valued 'cool' over 'good-looking' or 'pretty.' Looks weren't my priority when I made Big Mama, 2NE1, or BIGBANG. This was how I did things for the past twenty years, but I wanted to try a different way this time. I wanted BLACKPINK to be a group that has the looks and the talent . . . It's hard to find people who can sing, dance, and are pretty at the same time. That's why it took so long." – *Yang Hyun Suk on the origins of BLACKPINK, quoted in* YG Life

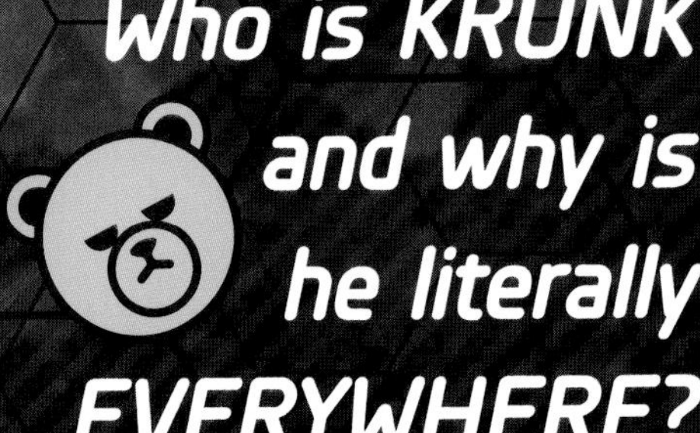

Who is KRUNK and why is he literally EVERYWHERE?

This blue bear is the swaggerific official mascot of YG Entertainment. He first appeared in YG artist Lee Hi's MV "It's Over," playing a boyfriend with attitude. He quickly made his way into the hearts, social media feeds, and MVs of everyone at YG. He even has his own blog, cafe, and video channel!

TRAINING TO BECOME THE NEXT K-POP SENSATION

Recruitment for BLACKPINK began in 2010, when YG held tryouts in several countries to find the best candidates for their next great K-pop girl group. Within months of passing the tryouts, Jennie, Jisoo, Rosé, and Lisa moved into the dorms with ten to twenty other girls and began their new life as pop star trainees.

They trained for twelve hours a day with one day off every two weeks. It was a hard adjustment. "I felt like it was a fight against myself," said Rosé in a Zach Sang interview. "Because it was really, really difficult being away from family, and I was so young. I had never slept outside of my house for more than two weeks at that age." Jennie chimed in, "Our whole life changed overnight."

Each month they competed in *American Idol*-style competitions, preparing a song and dance performance as groups and as individuals, and getting judged on their performances. Afterward, they would find out who came out on top and who was leaving. "To see some of the girls that I trained with go home just made me more motivated, because we all had one dream," said Jennie.

The girls would constantly be regrouped with different singing and dancing partners—and even different roommates. The producers tried out different combinations, trying to get just the right mix of sound, visual, and chemistry.

Eventually, four trainees stood out above the rest. In July 2016, YG released a video of BLACKPINK's dance practice, calling the group a "perfect harmony between 'sexy, powerful, and unique.'" The internet went wild and YG knew they had found the recipe for K-pop success.

In an interview with Soompi, BLACKPINK said that when girls were sent home, it made them practice harder, saying, "We came here for a reason, and thought it would be such a shame if we weren't able to realize our dream. So we resolved not to give up and went on."

In K-pop, members of a group are often assigned different roles by their entertainment companies. There is usually a leader, who is the oldest or the member with the most training. BLACKPINK does not have a designated leader. The main vocalist usually sings the most, which is Rosé. The main rapper is Jennie, and the main dancer is Lisa. Jisoo has been assigned the role of visual, which is the most attractive or distinctive-looking member.

BLACKPINK's training by the numbers:

Jennie	*recruited at 14*	*6 years as a trainee*
Lisa	*recruited at 14*	*5 years as a trainee*
Jisoo	*recruited at 16*	*5 years as a trainee*
Rosé	*recruited at 15*	*4 years as a trainee*

IDOL LIFE

While they met as competitors, the members of BLACKPINK now feel closer than family. They spend most of their sleeping and waking hours together. And whenever they have time off, the girls can often be found spending the day together, including a 2019 trip to Universal Studios in California.

When they debuted in 2016, YG head Yang Hyun Suk said, "Among the candidates, these four were the closest. I think this is the most important thing. The members have to get along. These four have been doing the monthly assessment together for a long time. Watching them, I thought they would make a good team together."

Idol Rules

They dance, they sing, they make intense MVs, they're fierce performers, they always look amazing, they always say the right thing at the right time, and they do it all with a big smile. As if that's not enough, most K-pop artists do it all under constant supervision and really strict rules imposed by their producers, such as . . .

NO

<DRINKING>
<SMOKING>
<DATING>
<TATTOOS>
<CLUBBING>

BLACKPINK House

In early 2018, the girls starred in a reality show called *BLACKPINK House*, giving fans a glimpse into their lives at home. *BLACKPINK House* follows the girls as they take a 100-day vacation in a pink-roofed house that was custom-made for them—complete with nearly fifty cameras to capture their every move. As trainees and as idols, BLACKPINK's lives are often in front of the cameras, but this was 24/7, even in their bedrooms.

The show, available for free viewing through BLACKPINK's official website, follows the girls as they enter the house for the first time, choose their rooms, and enjoy life in a house built just for them! "We lived together for over five years now. We played together a lot when we were trainees, when we had a lot of time," said Jennie. "Now we need our own space, so we spend our time individually." Which viewers see on the show.

These besties know everything about one another and fans have mashed them together in various combos, like *Lisoo* for Lisa and Jisoo, *Chaesoo* for Rosé and Jisoo, or even *JenChuLiChaeng*, combining all four girls' given names together.

BLACKPINK NEIGHBORHOOD

BLACKPINK FOLLOW

The house where *BLACKPINK House* was filmed used to be the Hello Kitty Café!

BLACKPINK FOLLOW

The Hongdae area, in Mapo-gu in Seoul, where BLACKPINK House was located, is a great shopping area, too.

BLACKPINK FOLLOW •••

Is it always a party in Hongdae?

BLACKPINK FOLLOW •••

Hongdae streets are busy day and night!

PRODUCER TEDDY PARK

Like YG's founder, Teddy Park started his career as a performer. He debuted in 1998 in the hip-hop group 1TYM, which recorded five albums over its influential career. In 2005, the group disbanded, and Teddy became an in-house producer for YG Entertainment. Teddy has a big influence on the label's sound.

At BLACKPINK's debut, Yang Hyun Suk praised Teddy. He said Teddy has "unwaveringly released many hit songs over the last twenty years. If Teddy were a designer, BLACKPINK is the amazing model and brand that he clothes with the newest and trendiest music."

The girls also appreciate how he's able to arrange music to reflect their personalities. "Before we complete our songs, we like our individual colors to be in the song," said Jennie. "Teddy is someone who has been watching over and guiding us for a long time, so he knows each of our strong points the best."

The members of the group rely on his expertise. "Teddy knows there are a lot of fan bases around the world that are just waiting on our songs, so I've seen him try to target those people," Rosé said. "Lisa spits out English raps, and e always comes up with cool phrases, because we're trying to take care of veryone listening to our music. I really respect that about our producer." He ven came up with the group's catchphrase, "BLACKPINK in your area."

October 2018, YG teamed up in partnership with US record companies niversal Music Group and Interscope Records to represent the group outside f Asia. Teddy was thrilled with the opportunity, saying, "Entertainment today more global than ever. Music and real talent transcends culture, language, nd really has no boundaries. Through this partnership we feel we can truly howcase BLACKPINK's potential on a grander scale and we look forward to vhat's to come."

While going to high school in the United States, Teddy decided he wanted to audition for YG Entertainment. When he was seventeen, he and his friend Taebin flew to Korea, had an audition, and were signed immediately. He returned to the US to finish high school, then moved to Korea, where he debuted in 1TYM in 1998.

DISCOGRAPHY

SQUARE ONE
August 8, 2016
(double A-side)
"Boombayah"
Producers: Teddy Park,
Bekuh BOOM (Rebecca Rose
Johnson)
MV Director:
Seo Hyun-Seung

"WHISTLE"
August 8, 2016
Producer:
Teddy Park
MV Director:
Beomjin J

SQUARE TWO
November 1, 2016 (double A-side)
"Playing with Fire"
Producer: R. Tee
MV Director: Seo Hyun-Seung
"Stay"
Producer: Teddy Park
MV Director: Han Sa Min

"AS IF IT'S YOUR LAST"
June 22, 2017 (single)
Producer:
Teddy Park
MV Director:
Seo Hyun-Seung

BLACKPINK
August 30, 2017 (Japanese EP)
"Boombayah"
"Whistle"
"Playing with Fire"
"Stay"
"As If It's Your Last"
"Whistle" (Acoustic)

RE: BLACKPINK
April 6, 2018
(Japanese EP reissue with new artwork and packaging)
"Boombayah"
"Whistle"
"Playing with Fire"
"Stay"
"As If It's Your Last"
"Whistle" (Acoustic)

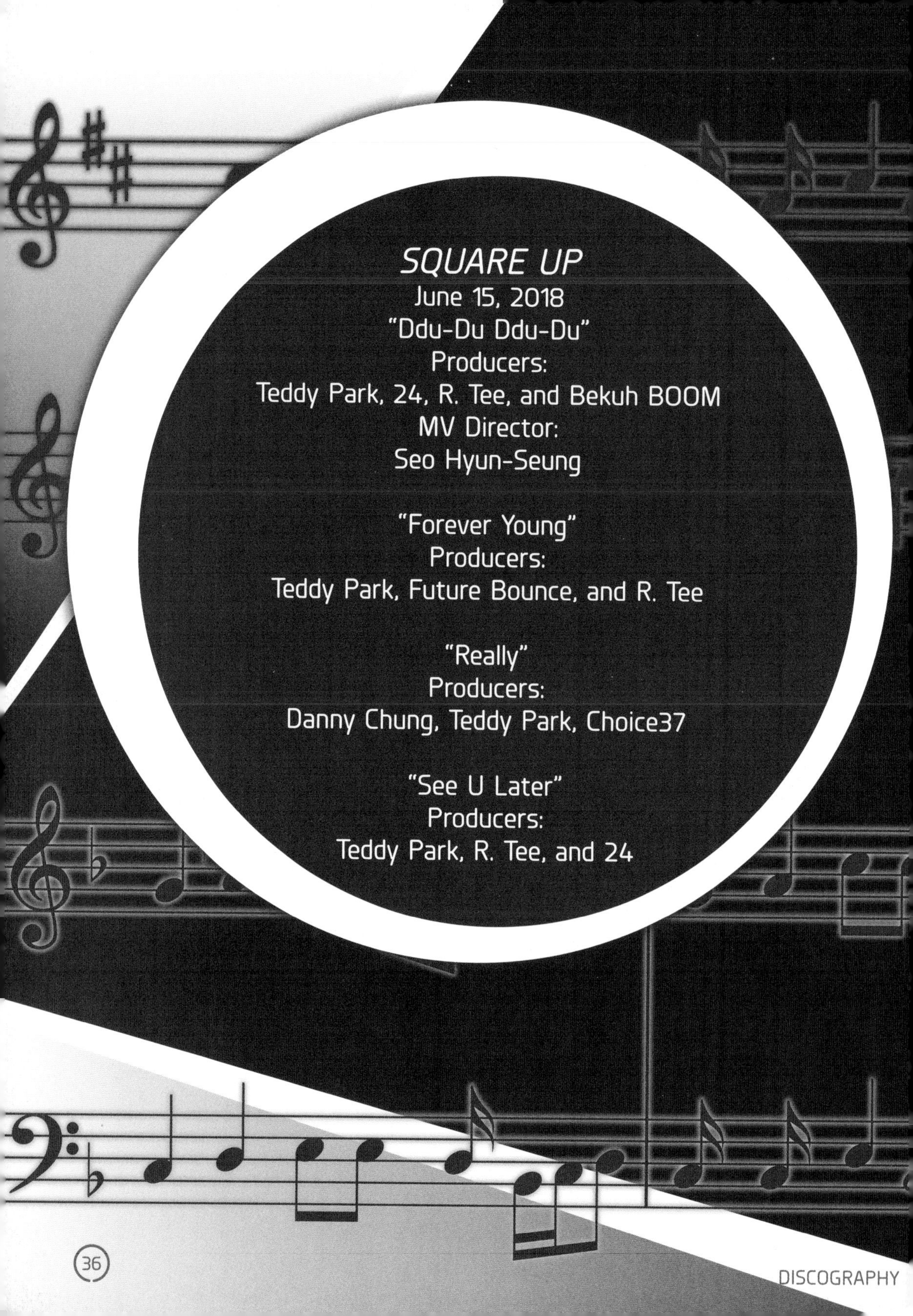

SQUARE UP

June 15, 2018

"Ddu-Du Ddu-Du"

Producers:

Teddy Park, 24, R. Tee, and Bekuh BOOM

MV Director:

Seo Hyun-Seung

"Forever Young"

Producers:

Teddy Park, Future Bounce, and R. Tee

"Really"

Producers:

Danny Chung, Teddy Park, Choice37

"See U Later"

Producers:

Teddy Park, R. Tee, and 24

YG head Yang Hyun Suk was initially hesitant about releasing "Ddu-Du Ddu-Du" as the title track of *Square Up*, but the girls felt it was the best choice. "My thoughts were the complete opposite of theirs. For Teddy and myself, the decision to use the song as the title track was a huge challenge and gamble," he said. "Compared to the songs that BLACKPINK has released so far, it's very strong and is rap-centered, so we thought it might not be mainstream enough." He added, "Although I was nervous, the one reason I was confident was the fact they had practiced more music that was closer to the 'black' than the 'pink' side of their name during their six years of being trainees, so I put my trust in the members."

"KISS AND MAKE UP"
October 19, 2018
(with Dua Lipa)
Dua Lipa (Complete Edition)
Producer: Banx & Ranx

"SOLO"
November 11, 2018
(Jennie's solo single)
Producers: Teddy Park, Park Hong-Jun, 24
MV Director:
Han Sa Min

BLACKPINK IN YOUR AREA

November 23 (digital), December 5 (physical), 2018 (Japanese studio album)

Disc 1
(in Japanese)
"Boombayah"
"Whistle"
"Playing with Fire"
"Stay"
"As If It's Your Last"
"Ddu-Du Ddu-Du"
"Forever Young"
"Really"
"See U Later"

Disc 2
"Boombayah"
"Whistle"
"Playing with Fire"
"Stay"
"As If It's Your Last"
"Ddu-Du Ddu-Du"
"Forever Young"
"Really"
"See U Later"

KILL THIS LOVE

April 5, 2019 (EP)

"Kill This Love"
Producers: Teddy Park, R. Tee, 24, and Bekuh BOOM
MV Director: Seo Hyun-Seung

"Don't Know What to Do"
Producers: Brian Lee, Teddy Park, 24,
Bekuh BOOM, and R. Tee

"Kick It"
Producers: Teddy Park, Danny Chung, TAEO, 24
MV Director: Seo Hyun-Seung

"Hope Not"
Producers: Masta Wu, Teddy Park,
Seo Won Jin, and Lydia Paek

Bekuh BOOM, one of the writers and producers on "Kill This Love," wrote that the song is "about being with someone you know is wrong for you and loving them so much it hurts you so badly to leave, but, at the same time, you know it would hurt more to stay." She goes on to say, "This song is about realizing that no matter how much you feel you love someone, if you know it's wrong for you, end it—kill it—because it is killing you inside."

SOLO

As BLACKPINK's star continued to rise, YG Entertainment announced that each of the four members of the group would be featured as solo artists. "We're always waiting to discover new parts of ourselves," Rosé says. "These solo projects are the biggest steps to discovering them."

In 2018, Jennie was the first to go it alone with her appropriately titled single "SOLO." "We all had to know how to perform on our own, that's always been there," says Jennie. "And when we started recording with Teddy, he said, 'You can't always depend on each other—you have to know how to fill up a song by yourself.'"

Jennie's solo debut dropped on November 12, 2018, and the world went wild. Her MV broke a record within the first twenty-four hours of its release, becoming the most viewed female K-pop solo artist

music video of all time. True to her passion for fashion, Jennie had more than twenty costume changes in just under three minutes, including a Burberry sweater, a Gucci leather biker jacket, and a pair of stiletto Yeezys. Within the first six months, Jennie became the first female South Korean soloist to break 300 million YouTube views, as well as the first to hit iTunes top 10 in the US. The hit song took the #1 slot in South Korea for two weeks in a row.

Jennie felt the experience helped strengthen the group. "I think by having solo projects, it allows us to expand our music range. There's a type of music and concept we can do as a group and do as solo artists," said Jennie to the Hollywood Reporter. "I think by working on both of these projects, our audience can get a fuller sense of us as artists, so I hope it benefits us both ways."

Jennie's outfits are specially constructed for lightning-fast changes.

Part of the group at Coachella.

Solo performance lets each member develop new aspects of her style.

Which member is up next? YG hasn't announced it yet, but the girls like the suspense. Jisoo said, "When people mention our solo projects, people start guessing: What will Rosé do? What *will Lisa do? I enjoy watching fans speculate."*

BLINKS

BLACKPINK is as dedicated to their fans as they are to their music. By sharing their lives through reality shows, social media posts, and live streams, the group members have created a bond with their superfans, called BLINKS, a word the group created that's a combination of "black" and "pink." During shows they light up the stadiums with their lightsticks. "Our fans bring them to represent themselves," said Rosé. "So when they are in a big crowd we can always identify our BLINKS."

These superfans have the power to create and distribute fanchants for audiences to sing at concerts, blow up Twitter in anticipation of BLACKPINK's appearances live and on TV "in your area," and even take to the internet to encourage YG Entertainment to expand their tour dates. BLINKS organize online pretty quickly when they're rallying around a cause, often prompting hashtags that trend within the first twenty-four hours of their creation, like the one they created for Jennie's birthday in 2018.

The girls are thrilled to find BLINKS all over the world. "All of our songs are in Korean [note: except for those translated to Japanese on *BLACKPINK IN YOUR AREA*, 2018 studio version], so I was really surprised that all these foreigners were singing along to a Korean song," said Jisoo. BLINKS also make each show special for the girls, often before the encore. "They try to make moments for us," Rosé says. "Fans throw a bunch of meaningful things [on stage]. Sometimes they throw a chipmunk [stuffed animal] because they think I look like a chipmunk! Or fan letters. Holding [those things] is just holding a part of them as well. It's great to see fans express themselves toward us . . . They try to make moments for us."

If you are comfortable reading and speaking Korean, you can become an official BLINK at blink.blackpinkofficial.com. But take heart if you can't join the official fan club. There are plenty of ways to keep up with these awesome artists and their fun and fabulous antics.

5 WAYS YOU CAN SUPPORT YOUR <3 of BLACKPINK ♥

1. See them in concert on their next tour.
2. Watch their MVs.
3. Download their songs.
4. Learn their dance moves.
5. Stay current with their style on social media by searching for the name of your bias plus "fashion" or "BLACKPINK fashion."

BLACKPINK's 2019 Los Angeles performance included "BLINKS Are the Revolution," a compilation video of their fans. It featured BLINKS of all ages singing and dancing to their favorite songs, including a scuba diver underwater with a sign that read, "Welcome to the Underwater Blink World."

Who is your bias? In the K-pop world, it's your absolute favorite celebrity—the one you support no matter what. For Rosé, her bias is the singer Halsey; she told Beats 1, "I love her voice; and she seems like the sweetest person ever." Jennie told ELLE Korea, *"My number one idol will always be Rihanna. She has everything I want to be."*

BLINKS

BLINKS

FANCHANTS

If you've ever attended a BLACKPINK concert in the United States, you've experienced the screaming mayhem of thousands of frenzied fans. The fans each express appreciation in their own way: waving lightsticks, blowing air horns, yelling out the artists' names during a quiet ballad, or just screaming at the tops of their lungs whenever they get excited.

The K-pop fandom, on the other hand, has a wonderfully choreographed but no less passionate way for fans to express their love: fanchants. At BLACKPINK concerts, BLINKS light up the stadium with both their pink hammer lightsticks and with their emotionally charged fanchants.

FANCHANTS IN YOUR AREA

While the YG Family does release fanchants, they change from region to region depending on the local language or what's trending. To find out the fanchant, you need to be in the know. Sometimes, local fan clubs hand them out or post them before BLACKPINK comes to town. Fans also post them online.

But some chants are universal. For example, when "Kill This Love" begins, fans shout out along with JenChuLiChaeng ***BLACKPINK in your area*** and in the chorus, fans repeat ***we lie***, ***so what***, and of course ***LET'S KILL THIS LOVE!***

For K-pop, one standard fanchant is to list all the members' full names from oldest to youngest:

BLACKPINK!
KIM JISOO
KIM JENNIE
PARK
CHAEYOUNG
LALISA
BLACKPINK BLINK!

BLACKPINK'S UNIQUE SOUND

Unlike a lot of current Western music, K-pop is defiantly upbeat. K-pop sensation BLACKPINK hits that beat head on. A large part of BLACKPINK's appeal is their intense anthems that contribute to their "girl crush" image. That directly feeds into the way the songs are written and structured—they're either swaggering kiss-offs or braggadocio. Several of their songs are led by heavy drops or compressed main riffs—"Kill This Love" and "Boombayah" are two examples. The kinds of things that just aren't often found in the songs on the American charts.

A softer song such as "Whistle" switches between acoustic break-downs and trap beats. The camp-fire jam "Stay" is largely an exception until Jennie and Lisa rap during a bridge. Their style has been described as "K-Trap," and while that's simplified, that genre blending may help explain BLACKPINK's appeal in America.

The BLACKPINK collaboration with Dua Lipa, "Kiss and Make Up," truly feels like the halfway point between the two acts. The song is as laid back and tropical-house inflected as most of Lipa's music, while including rapping and the distorted riffs that feel like the group's signature.

BLACKPINK's goal has always been world domination. It helps that Jennie, Rosé, and Lisa can speak fluent English and that YG Entertainment's roots in hip-hop keep them in touch with Western music's rap-dominated culture. Plus, each song is catchier than the last, and their catalog is accessible enough that there isn't a huge barrier for entry. Their appearances at major festivals, including Coachella, are proof of this. You don't have to understand everything about K-pop to listen to BLACKPINK; you just have to like extravagant, energetic music.

MV / MUSIC VIDEOS

BLACKPINK drops a music video every time they release a single. True to K-pop form, each one is a mash-up of costume changes and different scenes strung together to form a dreamlike story. The symbolism in each MV is open for fans to interpret as they wish. "Whistle," for example, features a car that doubles as a fish tank, two members sitting in a mansion with a dried-up tree between them, and each of the members singing while sitting on top of a spinning planet.

The girls often say in interviews that BLACKPINK has no "leader." This comes across in their music videos, where each member is featured in each song. Here are a few highlights from their MVs:

"Boombayah" (붐바야), 2016
(directed by Seo Hyun-Seung)

The first K-pop music video to surpass 600 million views on YouTube.

The MV for "Boombayah" served as an introduction to BLACKPINK's music, members, and vibe. The MV hits us with a contrast between the band's pink schoolgirl innocence and their rebellious, edgy lyrics and athletic dance moves. "BLACKPINK in your area" starts the song, then each member is introduced through a solo spotlight: Jisoo's glamorous side is contrasted with Lisa's playful vibe, Jennie's edge, and Rosé's sweet singing voice.

"Ddu-Du Ddu-Du" (뚜두뚜두), 2018 (directed by Seo Hyun-Seung)

The first K-pop group MV to reach 800 million views on YouTube.

This MV is more than just a fierce, trap-infused riot of color and costume changes. Jisoo told *Billboard* that her scenes in the MV represent current celebrity culture. "I'm wearing a pink wig, standing in front of a huge photo of me on the wall," she says. When she trips, all of the cameras turn toward her. "The message is about how people can go crazy about the celebrity figures and how they will aim at the celebrities if they make mistakes. We wanted to portray a scene that is interesting and meaningful to us."

"Kill This Love," 2019 (directed by Seo Hyun-Seung)

Most viewed video debut on YouTube, with 56.7 million views in the first twenty-four hours, and fastest to reach 100 million views. It got there in just three days.

In a surprising move, South Korean television channel KBS banned the crazy-popular video. It refused to play the video because there is a scene where Rosé is driving a car and she is not wearing a seat belt. This is a traffic violation in South Korea, and KBS felt that the video would promote unsafe driving.

Other BLACKPINK MVs with more than 300 million views on YouTube*:

- "Whistle" (휘파람), 2016 (directed by Beomjin J)
- "Playing with Fire" (불장난), 2016 (directed by Seo Hyun-Seung)
- "As If It's Your Last" (마지막처럼), 2017 (directed by Seo Hyun-Seung)
- "SOLO," 2018 (directed by Han Sa Min)

** As of May 14, 2019, Source: YouTube*

THE MOVES

When the girls were training to become stars, they spent long hours in the practice room, working with dance teachers and choreographers. All of that work has paid off, as their moves have been described as sexy, hypnotic, and explosive.

In a Los Angeles radio interview in April 2019, the girls explained that the move that's most fun to watch is surprisingly also their most challenging.
Rosé: The hair flips are the hardest.
Jennie: It hurts!
Rosé: You just have to let it go.

Lisa, the Dancing Machine

In their trainee days, the girls had dance competitions with other potential group members. The girls would get graded on their performances. Jennie recalled that Lisa would get straight As on every performance. The girls all agree that dancing comes most naturally to Lisa. Jennie compares Lisa's brain to a computer when she's learning a new dance move—she sees it once and can perform it instantly.

While the girls don't stick as closely to their group roles as most K-pop idols—they trade off on lead vocals in the group—Lisa is clearly the featured dancer.

Parris Goebel

Parris Goebel, also known as Parri$, is a choreographer, dancer, singer, director, and actress from New Zealand. Her dance crew, the Royal Family, are three-time winners of the World Hip Hop Dance Championship. She starred in Justin Bieber's "Sorry" MV. She also choreographed BLACKPINK's 2016 breakout dance practice video that they released to announce their debut as a group. The video featured the girls dancing in front of a mirror and a small audience to a song by Rihanna.

Kyle Hanagami

Kyle Hanagami is an American choreographer for many US artists, including Jennifer Lopez, Nick Jonas, and Ariana Grande, as well as for fellow K-pop superstars BTS. He has choreographed four BLACKPINK videos, including "Ddu-Du Ddu-Du," "Playing with Fire," and "Boombayah," and worked with New Zealand-based British choreographer Kiel Tutin on "Kill This Love." When working with them on "Playing with Fire," he tweeted, "BLACKPINK always smashes my choreography. First Boombayah, now this . . . these girls are on fire."

Kiel Tutin

Kiel Tutin began his career performing with and teaching New Zealand dance crews, including Parris Goebel's Royal Family. Since then, Kiel's worked around the world and with superstars such as Jennifer Lopez and Taiwanese star Jolin Tsai. When the "Kill This Love" MV set YouTube records, he tweeted, "I love being able to create with these ladies, this outro section was especially fun." The YG Family also released a video of Kiel and Lisa dancing to DJ Snake's song "Taki Taki."

BLACKPINK Style

Each member of BLACKPINK has a high-budget wardrobe peppered with major worldwide brands like Chanel, Louis Vuitton, Adidas, Coach, Puma, and Michael Kors. Their fans know which designers they're favoring in each video and even what shade of lipstick the girls are wearing. Their style is not only crush-worthy, it's also accessible.

While each member has her own unique vibe, their overall look is a mix of street style and schoolgirl sensibility with a luxury edge. Mixed in are elements from various eras, from 1980s Madonna bustiers and sequins to soft 1970s ruffles and floral prints to 1990s skater fashion. The overall effect is eye-catching high glamour.

To keep up the glam aesthetic, YG connected their stylists with designers like Chanel (which sponsors Jennie), Alexander McQueen, and Balenciaga. Top brands see a spike in their popularity when the BLACKPINK girls are spotted wearing their styles.

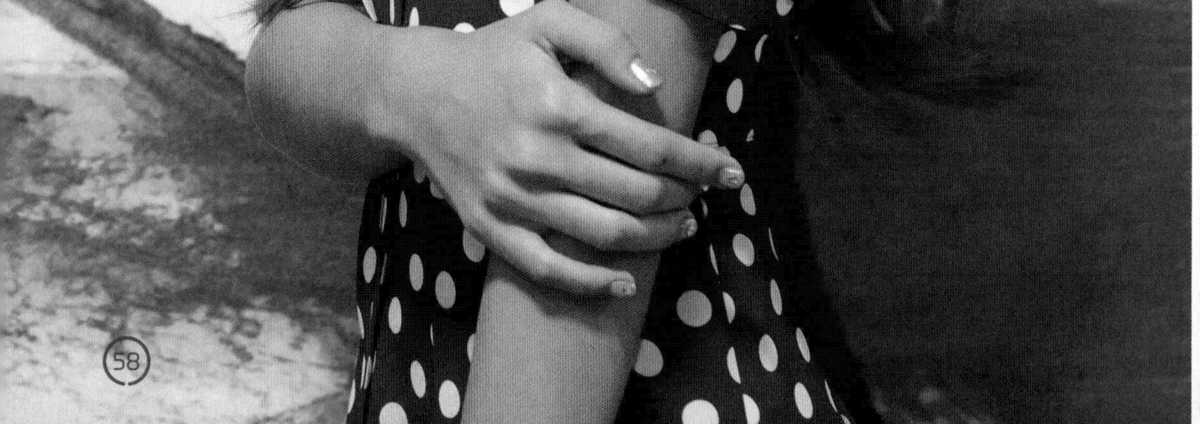

THE LOOK:

BLACKPINK *Style*

LISA

Lisa's unique style has a sporty edge with designer labels.

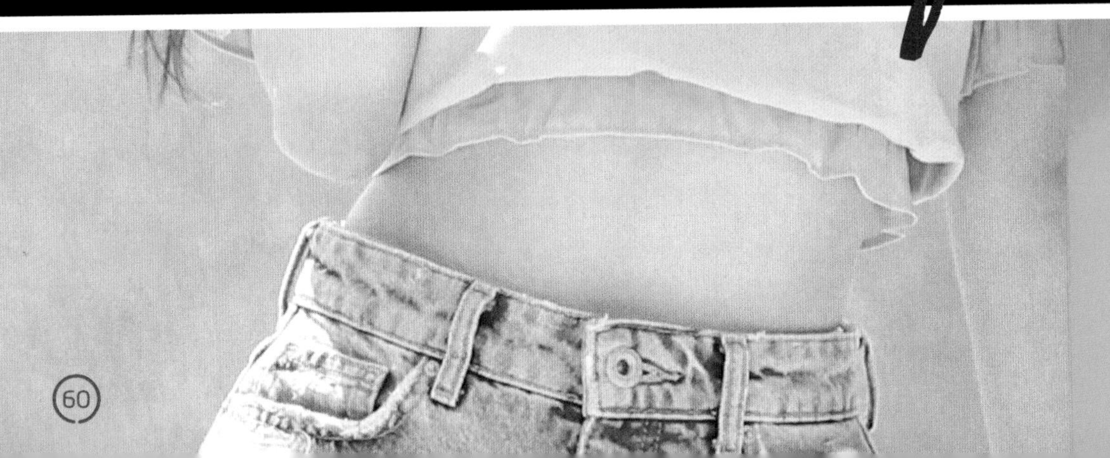

THE LOOK:
BLACKPINK *Style*

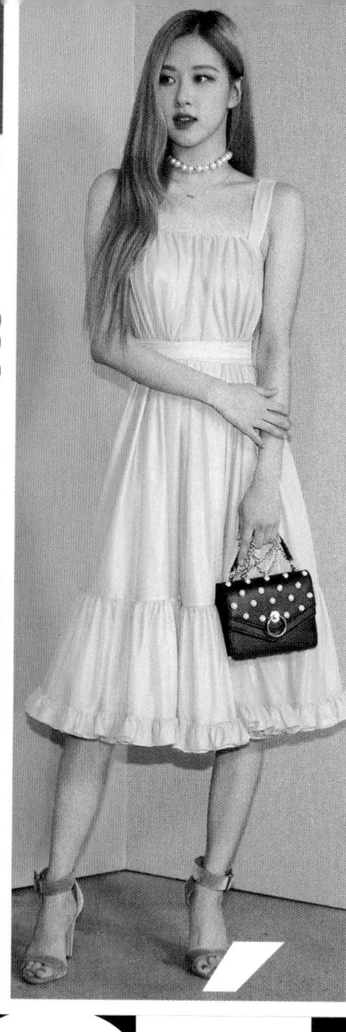

ROSÉ

Rosé's hippie-chic look often has her sporting ruffles and vintage street fashions.

THE LOOK: BLACKPINK Style

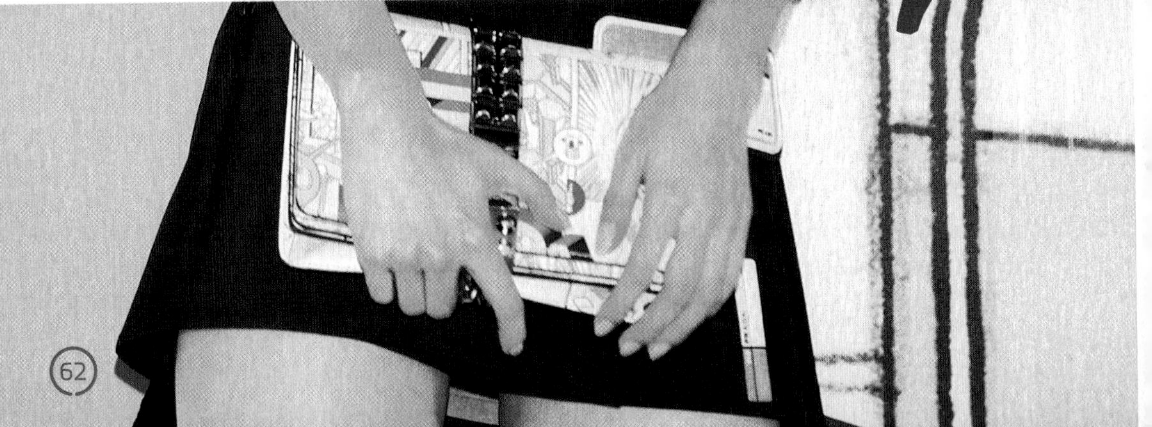

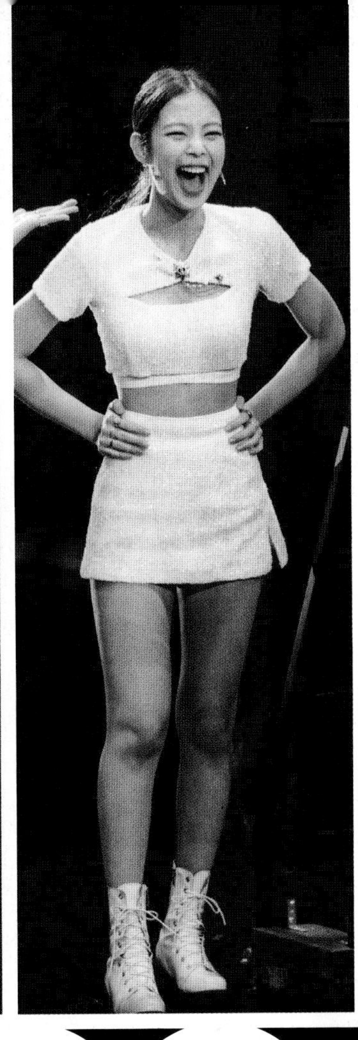

JISOO

Soft, glamorous, and always classy, Jisoo looks at ease whether she's onstage, playing video games, or just hanging out with the girls.

THE LOOK: BLACKPINK *Style*

JENNIE

Jennie is a fashionista with a closet full of clothes. While most of the things she wears these days are styled for her, Jennie admits that most of the clothes in her personal closet are black.

THE Stylists Behind the Fashion Revolution

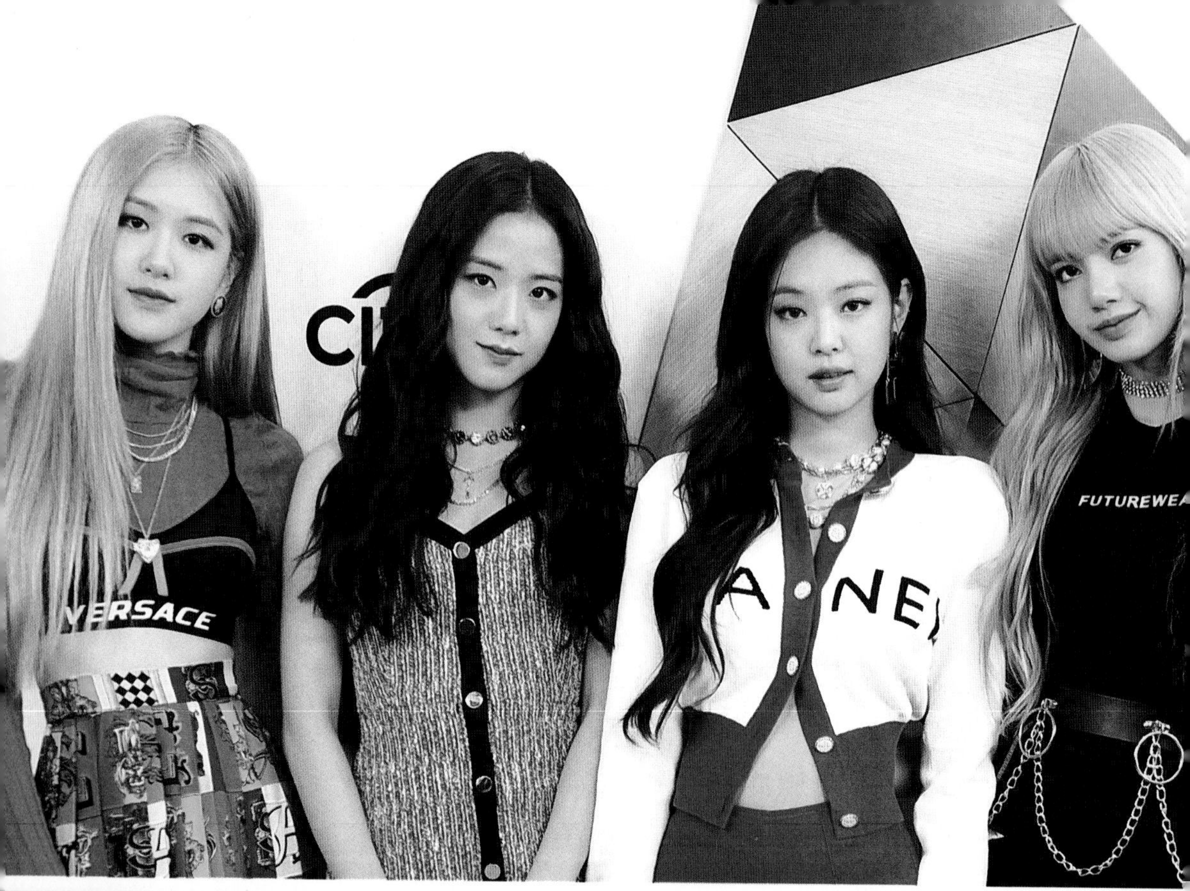

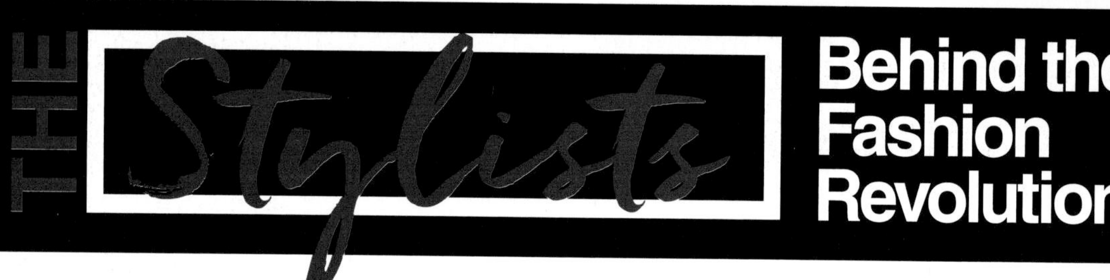

CHOI KYOUNG WON

As BLACKPINK's stylist since their debut in 2016, she defined the group's original style with one purpose in mind: to create something different that would become the definition of fashion in South Korea. *WWD* called the group's style a "chaotic mix of what's trending in luxury, novelty, and the underground—with a dose of cuteness for good measure." Won said of BLACKPINK's style: "The group is more loved by people who follow fashion. They are for an in-the-know girl."

JI EUN

Ji Eun is YG Entertainment's visual director, outfitting several other YG artists in addition to BLACKPINK. In 2019, she won the Style of the Year award during the Gaon Chart Music Awards—a major South Korean music awards show. In outfitting BLACKPINK for the "Ddu-Du Ddu-Du" MV, she told the K-pop culture magazine Soompi that she was aiming for a "girl crush vibe" where the artists' personalities determined each one's personal style. "Breaking away from their usual pretty image, it was hard to tell how far the powerful concept should go," said Ji Eun. "We did so many fittings."

For "Ddu-Du Ddu-Du," Ji Eun styled Jennie in a Dolce & Gabbana rainbow-striped chiffon gown with a rainbow corset belt. Rosé wore a tulle off-shoulder minidress from Parisian designer Y/Project. Jisoo's classy image was shored up by an Yves Saint Laurent playsuit in multicolor floral and gold lamé print. And Lisa's sporty, eclectic vibe came through as she accessorized her outfit with Balenciaga white knife-spike leather pumps and Chanel water-drop earrings.

JENNIE—HUMAN CHANEL

"Since Chanel is a brand I've admired for a long time, the nickname 'Human Chanel' was a bit burdensome at first. I thought it would be amazing if I get an opportunity to work with the brand Chanel even just once, but it became a reality and I feel grateful and happy that people say I match well with Chanel." —Jennie in *YG Life*

"The members are really pretty, so it was a lot of fun working with them. They were able to pull off anything."
—Ji Eun in Soompi

BLACKPINK Takes Tokyo

LACKPINK is known throughout Asia as "The Next-
eneration Girl Crush." In 2017, BLACKPINK was featured
both of Japan's major runway shows. They sang, danced,
d emceed Tokyo Girls Collection, one of the two biggest
shion events in Japan, in September 2017. They also closed
ıt the final set at the Kobe Collection—the other major
shion event in the area—to thunderous applause.

OME FASHION NAMES THAT HAVE AIRED UP WITH BLACKPINK

- LOUIS VUITTON
- PUMA
- REEBOK
- SHIBUYA 109
- TOKYO GIRLS COLLECTION X CECIL MCBEE
- ST. SCOTT LONDON
- CHANEL

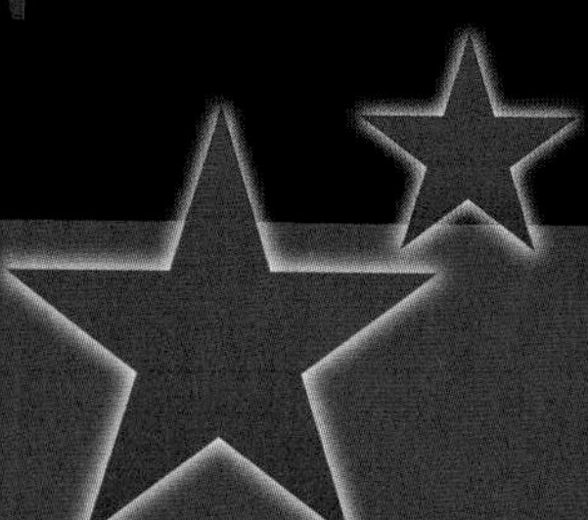

NONFASHION BRANDS

- KIA
- SHOPEE
- SPRITE KOREA
- SAMSUNG
- AIS TELECOM THAILAND
- WOORI BANK

COSMETICS

- HERA
- KISS ME
- DIOR COSMETICS
- MOONSHOT

There are several accounts online devoted just to break down the girls' style—who they're wearing and how the pairing it—as well as tips on how to mimic their l

THE GIRLS HIT COACHELLA

Sahara Tent, Coachella, Indio, California, April 12 & 19, 2019

BLACKPINK made history as the first K-pop female group to play the Coachella Valley Music and Arts Festival, an indie festival held each year in California's Colorado Desert. The show was their first full-length concert in the United States, and they weren't sure if the SoCal audience would be familiar with the group.

"We didn't expect to have such a big crowd and they were really singing their lungs out," said Jennie in a radio interview after the show. Rosé chimed in, "That was like the best part of it, was that we didn't expect it . . . It took me the whole hour to realize that everyone there was looking at us, that they weren't there for a different show."

In the eleven-song set, the group ran through all their hits, including Jennie's performance of "SOLO," as well as leading the crowd through two rounds of the wave.

"I have to say, when I was performing at Coachella, it was the most intense one hour of my life. It was just too much energy from everybody. I couldn't handle it."
—Jennie, the Zach Sang show

During the show, Rosé addressed the crowd, saying, "Us coming all the way from South Korea, we didn't know what to expect, and obviously we—you guys and us—we're from totally different worlds. But tonight I think we've learned so deeply that music brings us as one. So I want to thank you guys tonight for sticking by to the end of the show. You guys are awesome."

COACHELLA SET LIST

- Ddu-Du Ddu-Du
- Forever Young
- Stay (Remix version)
- Whistle
- Kiss and Make Up (Dua Lipa & BLACKPINK)
- SOLO (Jennie solo)
- Kill This Love
- Don't Know What to Do
- Kick It (Live debut)
- See U Later

Celebrities who were spotted hanging out with BLACKPINK at Coachella: *Will Smith, Jada Pinkett Smith, Jaden Smith, Willow Smith, Ariana Grande, Billie Eilish, Khalid, Diplo, Nina Dobrev, Kanye West, and more!*

In recognition of their massive popularity on the site, YouTube broadcast BLACKPINK's Coachella 2019 performance on the biggest billboard in New York City's Times Square, known as "The Beast," which is eight stories tall and spans the entire block from 45th Street to 46th Street on Broadway. This was the first ever live broadcast of a festival in Times Square.

COACHELLA

COACHELLA

COACHELLA

"You know how people say that after you go on a stage where you feel like you really interacted with a crowd, it lasts for a long time and it's really addictive? I totally experienced that [after Coachella]. After the show, we drove back to LA. I was in the hotel room, replaying it over in my head again and again. That was like the best feeling I have ever felt in my twenty-two years of existence."

—Rosé on the Zach Sang Show

BLACKPINK TIMELINE OF TRIUMPH

7/6/16 YG Entertainment unveils a dance practice video of new girl group BLACKPINK.

8/8/16 BLACKPINK releases *Square One*, a double A-side single with "Boombayah" and "Whistle." The same day, they release the "Whistle" MV.

8/14/16 BLACKPINK has their television debut, performing "Boombayah" and "Whistle" on South Korean music program *Inkigayo*. *Inkigayo* is a long-running South Korean TV show that airs live on Sunday nights and features performances by popular artists. The show also lists the most popular songs each week, calculating each song's popularity by combining digital sales, album sales, YouTube views, and advance votes. BLACKPINK won first place in the competition, making them the fastest artists ever to win after their debut.

8/2016 BLACKPINK's debut MV "Whistle" reaches 10 million views in its first five days.

1/4/17 "Whistle" reaches 300 million views on YouTube.

1/11/17 Jisoo and Rosé stun the audience of popular South Korea variety show *Radio Star* by singing a version of Justin Bieber's "Love Yourself" in English, backed by Rosé on acoustic guitar.

1/13/17 BLACKPINK wins Best New Artist of the Year at the 31st Golden Disc Awards, a music awards ceremony for the South Korean music industry.

1/14/17 BLACKPINK gives fans their official name: BLINKS, a mash-up of "black" and "pink."

1/19/17 BLACKPINK wins Best New Artist of the Year at the 26th Seoul Music Awards.

2/22/17 BLACKPINK wins the Song of the Year and Artist of the Year at the 6th Gaon Chart Music Awards.

6/20/17 "Whistle" makes an appearance on a season 1 episode of *The Bold Type*, a Freeform TV series. The song plays with English and Korean lyrics alongside a montage scene of characters planning their evening.

6/22/17 "As If It's Your Last" is released. It hits more than 13 million views on YouTube in 24 hours and debuts at #1 in 18 countries on iTunes.

7/16/17 BLACKPINK wins first place on *Inkigayo* for "As If It's Your Last" for the third time, earning the Triple Crown award. After an artist wins the Triple Crown achievement, they are no longer thought of as rookies.

7/20/17 BLACKPINK appears on Japan Premium Debut Showcase, Nipon Budokan, Tokyo, Japan.

8/29/17 BLACKPINK releases their self-titled EP in Japan, which debuts at the top of both the daily and weekly charts there.

Elle Magazine celebrated BLACKPINK's Japan debut in August 2017 with a super-glamorous music video of the girls trying on Rouge Dior liquid lip color, set to the English and Japanese version of "Boombayah."

Looking to recreate their fabulous lips? Rosé wore Frenetic Satin #788, Jisoo sported Spicy Metal #375, Jennie wore Fury Matte #265, and Lisa wore Crush Matte #272.

10/1/17 The group performs at Korea Music Festival.

11/17/17 The movie *Justice League* features the MV and song "As If It's Your Last" in the background in the Flash's Central City apartment.

12/15/17 "As If It's Your Last" YouTube music video hits 200 million views in the shortest time in K-pop history.

6/15/18 *Square Up* mini-album drops. It reaches #40 on the Billboard 200 on June 30.

6/15/18 "Ddu-Du Ddu-Du" is released as a single. The song debuts at #55 on the Billboard Hot 100 chart, goes on to top US Billboard's Billboard 200 and Hot 100 and UK Official Chart's Singles Top 100, and receives more than 100 million views on YouTube. For six months after its release, the music video for "Ddu-Du Ddu-Du" averages 2.5 million views per day.

7/7/18 "Ddu-Du Ddu-Du" wins Triple Crown on *Inkigayo.*

7/24/18–8/26/18 BLACKPINK Arena Tour—seven shows in Japan. The shows feature the songs from both the *BLACKPINK* and *BLACKPINK In Your Area* albums in Korean, English, and Japanese. The band also performs covers in English, Japanese, and Korean of artists such as Halsey, Beyoncé, Frankie Valli, Taeyang, and Wonder Girls. The performance also includes solo performances from each of the four BLACKPINK members.

BILLBOARD'S HOT 100

The Billboard Hot 100 list looks at the popularity of all songs across all kinds of music—country, rock, hip-hop, rap, pop—in the US. In just ten months, from June 2018 to April 2019, BLACKPINK hit the Billboard Hot 100 list with three songs:

"Ddu-Du Ddu-Du"
Peaked at #55 on 6/30/18

"Kiss and Make Up" (Dua Lipa & BLACKPINK)
Peaked at #93 on 11/3/18

"Kill This Love"
Peaked at #41 on 4/20/19

Before June 2018, the last time an all-female K-pop group hit the Hot 100 list was Wonder Girls with their song "Nobody" in 2009.

The girls talked with Zach Sang about the origin of "Kiss and Make Up." "Dua Lipa came to Korea for a show," said Jennie. "Me and Lisa went down, watched the show, and met her. She was so cool about it, she was like, 'I've heard of BLACKPINK, let's do a song together.' After a year, she sent us 'Kiss and Make Up.' Ta-da!" The girls loved it. "She hit us up with like the best song ever," said Rosé. "We were like, 'Yessss!'"

8/16/18 BLACKPINK is the first Korean group to receive a YouTube Diamond Play Button for having 10 million subscribers.

10/19/18 BLACKPINK and Dua Lipa release collaboration song "Kiss and Make Up."

10/23/18 BLACKPINK signs global record deal with Universal Music Group and Interscope Records.

10/2018 "Kiss and Make Up" (w/Dua Lipa) tops the music charts in twenty-one different countries, reaching #8 in the US, #26 in the UK, and #93 on the Billboard Hot 100 chart.

11/10/18–3/3/19 2019 BLACKPINK World Tour (In Your Area) in Asia.
BLACKPINK World Tour (In Your Area)—Sample Set List:

"Ddu-Du Ddu-Du"
"Forever Young"
"Stay" Remix
"Whistle"
"Clarity"—Jisoo solo (in Korean)
"Intro" + "Take Me" + "Swalla"—Lisa solo
"Let It Be" + "You & I" + "Only Look at Me"—Rosé solo
"SOLO"—Jennie solo
"Kiss & Make Up"
"So Hot"*/"Kill This Love"/"Don't Know What to Do"
"Playing with Fire"
"Really" Reggae Version
"See U Later"
"16 Shots"**/"Playing with Fire"
"Boombayah"
"As If It's Your Last"

ENCORES
"Ddu-Du Ddu-Du"
"Stay"***/"Hope Not"

* The North American tour replaced "So Hot" with "Kill This Love" and "Don't Know What to Do," as those songs were released after the Asia tour had ended.
** The Asia tour featured "16 Shots," but replaced it with "Playing with Fire" once the new album, *Kill This Love*, was released.
*** Performances on the Asia tour encore would end with "Stay," while the North American tour's second encore ended with "Hope Not."

11/13/18 Jennie's "SOLO" is released and debuts at #1 on iTunes Charts in forty countries, and tops the Billboard World Digital Song Sales Chart two weeks later.

2019

BLACKPINK's brand reputation skyrockets in 2019. The Korean Business Research Institute releases monthly rankings of brands across various categories. They find that in the first two months of 2019, BLACKPINK held the top spot of all girl groups, with the highest-ranking terms related to their name including "cute," "warm," and "love."

1/21/19 "Ddu-Du Ddu-Du" MV becomes the most watched K-pop video on YouTube, surpassing BTS's song "DNA."

4/5/19 BLACKPINK is the first worldwide girl group to top the iTunes chart since Destiny's Child fifteen years previously.

4/9/19 "Kill This Love" MV earns 56.7 million views in the first twenty-four hours.

4/12/19 BLACKPINK is the first all-female K-pop group to perform at Coachella.

4/15/19 Lisa reaches 17.4 million followers on Instagram, the most followed K-pop idol.

4/17/19–5/8/19 2019 BLACKPINK World Tour (In Your Area) in United States. BLACKPINK kicks off their US tour in Los Angeles and makes their way across the country, hitting a few national TV shows along the way, including *Good Morning America*, *Strahan and Sara*, the *Late Show with Stephen Colbert*, and the *Late Late Show with James Corden*.

4/20/19 "Kill This Love" peaks at #24 on the Billboard 200.

5/1/19 BLACKPINK and Dua Lipa surprise fans in Newark, New Jersey, with their first live performance together onstage.

5/6/19 BLACKPINK takes home the Shorty Award for best work by a music group in social media, beating out Harry Styles, Kacey Musgraves, Post Malone, Janelle Monáe, and Mason Ramsey. The award recognizes their amazing achievement of amassing a major following across their social media channels and producing exceptional content on Twitter, Facebook, YouTube, Instagram, and the rest of the social web.

5/7/19 "Kill This Love" MV reaches 300 million YouTube views, the fastest of any K-pop group.

5/18/19–5/28/19 2019 BLACKPINK World Tour (In Your Area) in Europe.

6/13/19–6/15/19 2019 BLACKPINK World Tour (In Your Area) in Australia.

7/13/19–7/14/19 2019 BLACKPINK World Tour (In Your Area) in Thailand.

BLACKPINK visits the *Late Late Show with James Corden!*

GIRLS & THEIR PETS

The members of BLACKPINK love their pets, who have been featured in their reality show and on social media. Jisoo has a dog, Dalgom, who perks up on air. "He's usually always sleeping," said Jisoo, "but I guess he's made for TV because he started to act up once I turned on the camera." Jennie has two dogs, Kumi and Kai, and has said, "My favorite thing to do is spend time with my dogs at the dorm." Lisa has four cats: Tiga and Hunter, who live in Thailand, and Leo and Luca, who live with her in Korea. "After I finish work for the day," she said, "I go back to the dorm and see my cats waiting for me and feel happy." Rosé has fish, one of which she's taught to do tricks.

JENNIE–DOGS

ROSÉ–FISH

LISA—CATS

JISOO—DOG

QUIZ: WHICH BLACKPINK MEMBER IS YOUR PERFECT MATCH?

1. What's your fashion vibe?
   a. Casual
   b. Elegant
   c. Glamorous
   d. Romantic

2. What are you having for dinner?
   a. Spicy Korean stew
   b. Almost anything with rice
   c. Thai food
   d. Kimchi

3. If you had an afternoon off, what would you do?
   a. Have an adventure
   b. Play video games
   c. Go shopping
   d. Play ukulele

4. What's your personality style?
   a. Sporty
   b. 4D (kooky)
   c. Nervous
   d. Chill

BLACKPINK BLACKPINK BLACKPINK BLACKPINK BLACK